W9-BDL-076

Bone-Chilling GHOST STORIES

BY JEN JONES

Consultant:
Simon Bronner
Distinguished Professor of American Studies and Folklore
Chair, American Studies Program
Pennsylvania State University, Middletown, Pennsylvania

Snap Books are published by Capstone Press,
1710 Roe Crest Drive, North Mankato, Minnesota 56003
www.capstonepub.com

Library of Congress Cataloging-in-Publication Data
Cataloging-in-publication information is on file with the Library of Congress.
ISBN 978-1-4296-9981-5 (library binding)
ISBN 978-1-4765-3559-3 (ebook PDF)

Editorial Credits
Angie Kaelberer, editor; Ashlee Suker, designer; Wanda Winch, media
researcher; Jennifer Walker, production specialist

Photo Credits
Alamy: Photos 12, 21; "An Authorized History of the Bell Witch by M.V.
Ingram, 1894", 11; Corbis: Jonathan Blair, 27; Flickr: cayobo, 7; The Myrtles
Plantation, 12; Painting by Dimitri Fouquet, 28; Shutterstock: A Cotton
Photo, 4–5, andreiuc88, back cover, 3, carlosdelacalle, 24, Doug Lemke, 15,
Elena Koulik, 17, ivanovskyy, 26 (right), keren-seg, 2, 6, 14, 20, Lario Tus,
cover (woman), Oleg Golovnev, cover (yellow brush stroke), prudkov, 4–5
(background), RomGams, 24–25 (background), SuperStock: Marsden Archive,
1, 19, 30–31; University of Pennsylvania: Online Books Page, McClure's
Magazine (Vol. 54, Number 1) via University of Michigan, Hathi, 10

Design elements:
Shutterstock: basel 101658, tree branch silhouette, David M. Schrader, brush
frame, Emelyanov, fractal pattern, foxie, brush stroke photo captions, grivet,
green texture, happykanppy, orange water color, hxdbzxy, creeper plant, Igor
Shikov, blue, red frame, javarman, tree frame, cloud background, kanate,
blue water color, Leksus Tuss, green scratch texture, Maryna Khabarova, ivy
castle wall, Massimo Saivezzo, grunge floral, yellow, mcherevan, chandelier,
mycteria, wood post, NinaMalyna, ornate black frame, optimarc, line brush
texture, pashabo, grunge green border, PeterPhoto123, smoke, Pixel 4 Images,
trees section, prudkov, purple landscape, branch design, Ralf Hirsch,
climbing ivy, Theeradech Sanin, distressed wood frame

Printed in the United States of America in North Mankato, Minnesota.
032013   007223CGF13

Table of Contents

Are Ghosts Real?

It's the million-dollar question: Do ghosts truly exist?

Hundreds of legends and reported sightings seem to point

to "yes." But many people still doubt whether life really continues

on the "other side."

From the sea to a cemetery to a farm, nowhere is safe from things that go "bump" in the night. Get ready to be totally …

Scared.

Chapter One

Family Curses

Robert the Doll

Four-year-old Robert Eugene Otto, known as Gene, was thrilled when his family's maid gave him a child-sized doll in 1904. Gene named the doll Robert.

Robert kept Gene company in his hometown of Key West, Florida. They wore matching sailor suits. Gene insisted that the doll sit next to him at the table. Gene's parents often overheard him talking and fighting with Robert, using a different voice for the doll.

One night Gene's dad was reading the newspaper and heard a terrifying cackle. "Gene, that's enough," he scolded.

Robert now lives in a museum.

But when Gene's dad turned around, Gene wasn't in the room. It was only the doll sitting on the couch. Gene's dad thought he must have imagined what he'd heard.

One night Gene's parents were awakened by a thud and Gene's screams. They rushed to his room and found a desk knocked over. Gene sat in the corner, shaking and pointing at Robert. "He did it!" Gene said. Robert lay on the bed. The corners of his mouth were turned upward in a creepy smile.

Things only got stranger from there. Gene's mom was in the kitchen one afternoon when she saw Robert run past the doorway. Later a neighbor reported seeing Robert floating outside the window while Gene's family was away. People began saying that the former maid had cursed the doll—and the family.

In 1930 Gene married Annette Parker. They lived in New York City for several years before returning to the family home in Key West. They spent the next 40 years there. Robert stayed with them—in his own room. Robert even went on trips with the couple. When Gene died in 1974, his wife placed Robert in the attic. She then sold the house. The home's next owners claimed that the doll terrorized their daughter. They quickly moved. The maid's curse not only outlived Gene but also took on a life of its own.

Today Robert the Doll is in a museum in Key West. Legend says museum visitors must ask the doll for permission to take its picture or risk being cursed forever.

For Whom The Bell Witch Tolls

When John and Lucy Bell moved from North Carolina to Tennessee in the early 1800s, things looked promising. Their new home had many acres of farmland next to the Red River. It became a wonderful home for the pair, who eventually had nine children.

One day in 1817, John was working in the cornfields when he spotted a strange animal. Before him stood a dog with a rabbit's head. He reached for his rifle and shot three times as the beast scampered away.

Later that evening, scratching and knocking noises were heard against the outdoor walls of the Bell house. The next night, the noises were heard inside the house. The children complained that it sounded like rats were chewing on their bedposts.

The invisible terror seemed focused on the Bell children, especially 11-year-old Betsy. During the night, it often ripped off the children's bedcovers and threw their pillows on the floor. At first their parents thought the children were making up the stories. But Betsy changed their minds.

John Bell's family gathered around him when he became ill.

Betsy ran screaming into their bedroom one evening. She insisted that the ghost had slapped her and pulled her hair. Lucy gasped as she comforted Betsy. A bright red handprint was still visible on Betsy's face.

For years the evil witch spirit haunted the family. The spirit whispered in their ears and terrorized Betsy's fiancé until he left her. The spirit's final revenge came in the form of John's death in 1820.

John's family found a small container near his body with a mysterious liquid inside. When they fed some of it to their pet cat, it died almost instantly. It was clear that John had drank the potion and been poisoned. John Bell Jr. quickly threw the container into the fireplace. The container burst into a blinding blue flame and vanished up the chimney.

No one knows why this evil spirit wanted revenge on the Bells, but it certainly achieved its goal. Today the legend is the inspiration for several movies and books. Beware the "Bell Witch!"

Betsy Bell was terrorized by the witch.

A Haunted Plantation

If you visit the Myrtles Plantation in St. Francisville, Louisiana, be warned. You could end up sharing your room with one of several ghosts that reportedly haunt the inn.

The most famous Myrtles ghosts is Chloe. According to legend, Chloe worked as a slave for plantation owners Clark and Sara Woodruff in the early 1800s.

Chloe's ghostly image is behind the far right pillar of the front porch.

The story says that Clark caught Chloe spying on him one day. He had one of her ears cut off as punishment. From that day on, Chloe wore a green head wrap to hide her scar.

Not long after the incident, the Woodruffs' oldest daughter had a birthday. Chloe baked a cake for the party. Some people believe Chloe poisoned the cake, killing Sara and two of the couple's children. However, records show that the three family members actually died of yellow fever.

No matter how the Woodruffs died, Chloe's fate was sealed. The other slaves were terrified of her. They hanged her from a tree and threw her body into the Mississippi River. They hoped that she would never be seen again.

Their wish wasn't granted. A crying ghost wearing a green head wrap can often be seen around the plantation. She's in good company. Guests have also seen ghostly children playing in the halls and a young girl floating outside a window.

If you want a peaceful vacation, you might want to stay somewhere else!

Chapter Two

Spooky Places

The Helpful Sea Captain

Even friendly ghosts can scare people. At Owl's Head Lighthouse in Maine, a sea captain's ghost is said to watch over the property. His footprints are often spotted in the snow. The lighthouse's brass fixtures are always a bit shinier after his appearances.

The first sighting happened in the mid-1980s, when Andy Germann was the Coast Guard lighthouse keeper. One night Andy went outside to gather some building materials. Later Andy's wife, Denise, thought that she felt him getting back into bed. But when she turned over, she saw the outline of an invisible person under the sheets.

The current lighthouse was built in 1852.

The next day, Andy told Denise that he'd seen a cloud of smoke float into the bedroom just before the ghostly sighting.

The Graham family took over at Owl's Head in 1987. Their 3-year-old daughter, Claire, moved into the room where the most ghostly activity had taken place.

Claire soon developed an imaginary friend. She described him as an old sea captain who had a beard and wore a blue coat and sailor cap.

One night Claire's imagination became all too real. She burst into her parents' room yelling, "Fog's rolling in! Time to put the foghorn on!" Claire said she'd gotten the message from her sea captain friend.

The Grahams finally got the message too. They left the lighthouse after just two years. Today Owl's Head is known as one of the top 10 haunted lighthouses in the world.

The Beautiful Stranger

The Hotel del Coronado in San Diego, California, is a place where all signs point to "ghost." Rooms suddenly get unbearably chilly. Strange sounds and smells abound. Footsteps can be heard when there are no people present. Lights and TVs flicker on and off randomly. Breezes blow even when windows are closed.

Trace the cause back to November 24, 1892, when a pretty young woman checked into room 312. She said her name was Lottie Bernard. Lottie told hotel employees that she had come from the Midwest to receive medical treatment. She appeared lonely and unhappy.

Five days later, Lottie's body was found on one of the hotel's back staircases near the beach. She had apparently shot herself in the head. Police searched her room for clues but failed to find many belongings. They sent a sketch of her face to newspapers and police stations all over the country. They hoped to find out more about her life.

The investigation revealed that Lottie's real name was Kate Morgan. She married an Iowa gambler named Tom.

One witness said that he'd seen Kate and Tom arguing on a San Diego-bound train days before the body was found. Tom had gotten off the train before reaching the city. No one knows why Kate decided to take her life. But many think it was because Tom never showed up at the hotel.

Kate's ghost still has a strong presence at the Hotel del Coronado. Ghost hunters flock there to try to get a glimpse of the lost soul known as the "Beautiful Stranger."

Kate's room at the hotel is now number 3327.

The Brown Lady

Life as a photographer can be glamorous and unpredictable. You never know just what you might capture in your lens. In 1936 photographers Hubert Provand and Indre Shira were taking photos at an English country home, Raynham Hall. That day their lives changed with one click of the shutter.

They were preparing to shoot the staircase when Shira saw a glowing veiled figure coming down the steps. Provand quickly snapped a photo. When the photo was developed, a ghostly figure appeared on the stairs. The photo is one of the most famous pieces of paranormal evidence.

The subject of the picture is "The Brown Lady." She was known in life as Lady Dorothy Walpole Townshend. Her husband was Charles Townshend, who was said to be an angry, violent man. He locked Lady Dorothy inside one of Raynham Hall's rooms. She was left to waste away for the rest of her life. She wasn't even allowed to see her children.

Since Lady Dorothy's death in 1726, many people have met her spirit. One was King George IV of Britain. He awoke to find Dorothy standing above his bed in a brown satin dress.

The image of a ghostly lady was photographed at Raynham Hall.

Another was writer Frederick Marryat, who stayed at the Hall for a few nights to test the ghost theory. He slept with a loaded gun under his pillow. When he saw the "Brown Lady" gliding down a hallway, he grabbed the gun and shot.

The bullet passed right through her.

Chapter Three

Famous Ghosts

A Ghostly Ship

Sailing the Cape of Good Hope off the South African coast is an awe-inspiring experience. That was the case for Captain Hendrick Vanderdecken, who braved its waters in the late 1600s. As the Dutch captain's ship sailed the Cape, he became lost in thought. He failed to notice the dark storm clouds rolling in from the west.

A clap of thunder boomed. Lightning crackled in the sky. The waters got choppy, and the rain began to pour. Captain Vanderdecken yelled for his crew.

Sailors report seeing a ghostly ship just before a storm.

The crew members began working to steer the ship to safety. For hours the ship tossed and turned on the waves. The soaked crew got a ray of hope when the rain slowed. The sea became slightly calmer. Then …

Crunch!

The ship made a horrible sound as it hit a giant rock sticking out of the water. The ship began to sink. Water flooded in through the hole created by the crash. The crew tried to fix the damage, but it was too late.

Captain Vanderdecken stood stunned by what had happened. He angrily vowed, "This boat will round the Cape even if we have to keep sailing until Judgment Day!"

The ship plunged into the water, drowning everyone on board. The last thing visible was the captain's fist thrust into the air. To this day, Captain Vanderdecken and his ship—known as the *Flying Dutchman*—haunt the seas. Sailors all over the world claim to see the glowing ship trapped in the eye of fierce storms.

Ghostly Sighting

In July 1881 Prince George of Great Britain was serving aboard the HMS *Bacchante*. The prince recorded that a lookout spotted the *Flying Dutchman* as the ship rounded the Cape of Good Hope. George later became king of Britain.

White Wolf

During summer 1872, a warm night in Lafayette, Indiana, provided the perfect opportunity for a bonfire. William Lingle had invited a group of people to a backyard party at his home. The guests included a British professor, two newspaper reporters, and a courtroom judge. The common thread? They were all fascinated by the supernatural.

The guests were eagerly listening to Lingle's story about a nearby haunted house built on an old brickyard. One man asked to see the haunted house. Everyone agreed, and off they went.

When they arrived, there were no traces of ghostly activity in the crumbling building. But the five men were patient. They sat in the rubble for hours, waiting for something to happen.

Suddenly, a bright blue light filled the room. When it faded, in its place was a white wolf. The wolf let out a deafening howl, pointing its head toward the sky. It then shape-shifted into a giant frog. The creature transformed yet again, this time into an American Indian man. The man then vanished.

The spirit took the form of a wolf.

The professor went back to Lingle's house. He returned with a giant metal wand. He used the wand to draw a circle in the dirt with a series of images inside. The rest of the men sat in amazed silence.

Smoke rose from the circle. When it cleared, the American Indian man stood before them. He had a tattoo of a froglike creature on his right arm. He spoke to the professor in a language no one else could understand.

The professor shared the story. The powerful man was once known as White Wolf. He had been buried on a nearby Indian reservation after his death. Yet his spirit had never been able to rest in peace. The city had begun to dig up the cemetery ground for new construction. White Wolf's ghost was doomed to roam Lafayette unless the cemetery was restored.

Today Sunnyside Middle School is located on the site of the ancient cemetery. No word on whether a white wolf roams the school's halls at night.

Shape-Shifters

White Wolf may have been a shape-shifter. Some Native American cultures believed that these spirits could take on the form of people or animals. The Navajo people called these restless spirits "skinwalkers." They believed that if a person looked deep into the eyes of a skinwalker, it could take over the person's body. The Navajo were said to avoid looking other people directly in the eyes.

A Tragic Queen

Being the Queen of England seems like a dream come true. But for Anne Boleyn, it was a nightmare. She and her husband, King Henry VIII, were deeply in love when they first met. But the king turned on Anne after she gave birth to a daughter. Henry wanted a son who could inherit the throne.

Less than three years after their daughter, Elizabeth, was born, Henry made a shocking move. He had Anne arrested and sent to the Tower of London. The king claimed that she had committed a number of crimes, including working against the government. Henry also said Anne was a witch who used her power for evil. Anne was found guilty in a court trial and sentenced to death.

On the day of her execution, May 19, 1536, Anne's faint smile showed that she had accepted her fate. Blindfolded, she knelt down as a swordsman cut off her head.

Anne was buried inside the Tower of London's chapel. But her ghost refuses to rest. On the anniversary of her death, she is said to appear at Blickling Hall, where she was born. Her headless ghost arrives in a coach pulled by six headless horses.

Anne Boleyn's body rests under the floor of the chapel.

Every Christmas Anne is seen wandering the grounds at
Hever Castle. King Henry once courted her there.

But the scariest Anne Boleyn sightings have happened at
the Tower of London. She often roams the site of her execution,
carrying her own head. Tower guards have been attacked and
even scared to death by sudden appearances of her ghost.

Voodoo Queen of New Orleans

Want to go where the ghosts are? Take a trip to New Orleans, Louisiana. It's said to be the most haunted U.S. city. Even running errands can turn into a scary experience! Just ask Elmore Lee Banks. In the 1930s, his trip to a drugstore on St. Ann Street became an unforgettable ghost story.

Banks was waiting at the counter. An old lady wearing a long white dress and a blue turban got in line beside him. Suddenly, the pharmacist's eyes bulged out of his head in fright. He fled to the back of the store to hide.

Marie was famous for her voodoo skills.

Confused, Banks turned toward the woman, who cackled

with laughter. "Don't you know who I am?" she asked.

"No," said Banks, growing more impatient by the minute.

The woman's eyes darkened with anger. She smacked a

stunned Banks hard across the face. She then flew through the

door and over the telephone wires into the neighboring St. Louis

Cemetery. Banks promptly passed out on the drugstore floor.

Banks woke up as the pharmacist tried to revive him.

"You know who that was?" said the pharmacist. Banks shook

his head. The pharmacist said the woman was the legendary

voodoo priestess Marie Laveau. She died in 1881. Her angry

ghost is said to
roam St. Louis
Cemetery with her
loyal boa constrictor
snake, Zombi.

"Son, you were
slapped by the
Queen of Voodoo!"

A Hair-Raising Job

During her lifetime,
Marie Laveau worked as
a hairdresser for wealthy
New Orleans women.
She used her job to find
out her clients' secrets
and provide voodoo
cures for their problems.

Finding Ghosts

Spooked yet? Based on these real-life tales, it's clear you don't need to be a ghost hunter to have a supernatural experience. You could find yourself face-to-face with an otherworldly visitor. If it does happen, write it down. Maybe your story will be passed down and told many years later ... leaving readers totally, completely ...

Scared.

READ MORE

Chandler, Matt. *The World's Most Haunted Places.* The Ghost Files. Mankato, Minn.: Capstone Press, 2012.

Everett, J. H. *Haunted Histories: Creepy Castles, Dark Dungeons, and Powerful Palaces.* Christy Ottaviano Books. New York: Henry Holt and Company, 2012.

Stone, Adam. *Haunted Houses.* The Unexplained. Minneapolis, Minn.: Bellwether Media, Inc., 2011.

INTERNET SITES

FactHound offers a safe, fun way to find Internet sites related to this book. All of the sites on FactHound have been researched by our staff.

Here's all you do:

Visit *www.facthound.com*

Type in this code: 9781429699839

Super-cool stuff! Check out projects, games and lots more at
www.capstonekids.com

OTHER TITLES IN THIS SET: